her uncomfortable fortune

Shelby L. LaLonde

Edited by Sheila M. Moon
Book Cover Created by Ruby Darling
@selfpubcovers.com © 2019

Her Uncomfortable Fortune/
Shelby L. LaLonde. -- 1st ed.
ISBN 978-1-7336785-2-0
ebook ISBN: 978-1-7336785-3-7
Library of Congress Control Number: 2019901913

I write for the sensitives.
The mystics and the poets.
Those of you who are connecting
to your intuition and inner guidance.
For the dreamers and the doers.
For the different, and the other.

No one can make you feel inferior without your consent.

—ELEANOR ROOSEVELT

Contents

THE GIFTS:

her uncomfortable fortune

THE RESERECTION:

the meeting of her past selves

THE DARKNESS:

the meeting of her shadow

THE INTEGRATION:

the merging of all her selves

THE RISING:

her Venus rising

A NOTE FROM YOUR STORYTELLER:

Walk with me,
as I set my secrets free.

accepting the gifts:

her uncomfortable fortune

MY ANGEL SHE CAME

I was just a little girl.

Teeny-weeny

and four years old.

The radio on

as we drove along.

I was singing,

quietly along.

I must have fallen

sweetly asleep.

I didn't hear the crash you know.

I just saw myself

a mess below.

Blood all over

what was my head.

I guess my dad thought I was dead.

He yelled out screaming, carrying me.

"Somebody help my baby!"

"Please!"

As I watched from up above,

I felt so strongly

all his love.

I wasn't crying or even scared.

I felt at peace,

to say the least.

I gazed on,

wondering what was wrong.

As I watched

my father's crying song.

When from behind me to my left,

it was an Angel

I could guess.

She guided me on then,

from behind.

I could feel her heart

blending with the mine.

She took me to see my family.

They were all okay,

all alive.

She was letting me know,

they had all survived.

From there she led me to the one in white.

The one who stood before the light.

Together,

they let me know I would get past this night,

as they took my soul to flight.

For what happened then,

it lingers in me.

It has been revealed to me slowly.

They showed me then,

what would be my life.

They told me that

I couldn't die that night.

That I was here for some great purpose,

that without me the world,

just might not make it.

They said I had made a promise before my birth.

Before my soul entered into the earth.

They showed me what I came here for.

It was something that my soul adored.

I felt the love

I have for all of you.

So I'll come back,

and show you I do.

I'll come back,

and tell you why.

I'll come back,

with this feeling inside.

They then took me back to my earthly house.

I slipped in quietly,

like a mouse.

I woke quickly from the deep.

My eyes never wider,

I felt all at peace.

Though I was crying,

they were stitching my head.

I was a child

and playing again.

If they hadn't been there to guide me that night,

I may have stayed.

I might not be here with you today.

A few years later,

a river I fell in.

I felt all that love,

and peace again.

I could breathe,

though water was all around.

Silence I heard

was the only sound.

My Angel she came again to my left side.

I was in her space.

It was open wide.

Together we watched the bubbles,

as they slowly rised.

I felt all the love

she had for me inside.

That time again

I could have died

without my Angel by my side.

I thank my Angels,

they've helped me to grow.

They continue to guide me and help me to know,

what is kept within my soul.

I hope you can feel something from my words.

It is my way,

to say what I must say.

I feel blessed to be here with all of you.

You are all in some way

my Angels too.

TREASURE

What if she's right?

What if there is a treasure kept?

One that only I protect?

Why do they want it?

What do they care?

What sort of power,

lies inside there?

Could they take it?

Would I know?

How do they see it?

What do I show?

SKIP

Grandpa died when I was 12 years old.

I remember his body lying there cold.

But I also knew,

something of souls.

I couldn't exactly define it though.

Because as a child,

I saw things,

most don't.

Though I cried,

I knew he didn't die.

Not his soul,

It was just his time

to let his body go.

Shortly thereafter

he started visiting me.

Came to help make sense

of all I could see.

Taught me about what I now know as,

vibration and energy.

Because before then,

I didn't know,

just why it was that some things glowed.

Or that it was really,

just a ghost.

I just knew that I wished I didn't see it.

In fact I pleaded to all that is,

to be free of it.

Or why it was,

that I sometimes froze,

when that specific question arose.

As if to answer,

was some sort of trap.

Something of which

I could never come back

with answers of how,

I could know something like that.

Or why I'd tell someone about a dream,

and later on

it would be seen.

I've learned a hundred ways to use my vision.

How to translate,

and to express

the impressions I'm given.

He taught me access

to my uniquely monotoned,

inverted wisdom.

Often called extrasensory,

or intuition.

Grandpa came,

he showed me eight fingers.

Eight days later,

Wendy died.

WENDY

It's as if she's birthing butterflies before my eyes.

Happy.

Awakening beautiful creatures on the other side.

Setting them free to discover all of life's

mysteries.

Though I miss her here dearly.

She's holding marvel within her hands.

Accomplished and willing,

she understands.

She never really did go away.

I just have to listen to her now,

in different ways,

to hear the things

she wants to say.

I'll know it's her,

because it's like I'm embodying her.

She'll draw me pictures or flash me a word,

to be sure the message she's sending,

can be heard.

Like a game of charades,

until I get.

Capture the feelings held within it.

She walks now with the ones in blue.

She walks with bells

the way they do.

Whispering wisdom and guidance to you.

They are the Magdalene's.

SHARP AND UNSAFE

Sharp and unsafe I feel today in this human place.

Like I could get cut

if I go outside.

Physically hurt by their false faded eyes.

All of their ills,

are making me sick.

To me their bullshit just sticks.

I can't choose or pick.

Today I just can't transmute any of it.

Can't contemplate it or move it away,

help anyone out of their pain today.

Can't listen to their remembrance

of things happened before

once more.

All the emotions undealt with they've carried.

The words they think,

yet left unspoken,

choosing to ignore,

their emotions once more,

and all their aims to settle said scores.

What they fling around without a care,

because they choose to remain unaware,

so that they don't *have* to care.

Their denial,

I almost envy.

No one wants to admit they're heavy.

I can't wait for them anymore to be ready.

So I guess it's inside

I'll choose to stay.

Keep away from the games being played.

I know I have to be careful

when I feel this way.

Totally cautious of what I may say,

because I'm not able

to fake anything away.

So vulnerable it is to be this open.

Understanding what and why it's broken.

Forever figuring up ways to save it.

I never really escape it.

EMPATHIC

What does it look like to always be so put

together?

I wouldn't know.

For I'm always chasing rabbits

down their holes.

Wandering through sounds,

of the voices of souls.

The whispers of everyone's winter's ya know.

Some people catch colds.

But I catch what's nestled,

deep within souls.

It's not mine.

It's his or it's hers.

The mailman's,

a movie,

or even a tree.

Every fear,

all tears,

soaked in by me directly.

Instantly,

I'm stepped into their stories.

Encased in a world where hearts never heal.

Where all I get to do is feel.

Sometimes I just can't deal.

Swimming in struggles

of emotional wheels.

THOUGHTS ARE THINGS

I follow thoughts into the consciousness that

makes up all of this.

They burst.

Then disperse from your heads like clouds.

What you think and how you mean it,

determines its direction,

shape,

and size.

I can see it's feelings.

Sometimes I'll catch its thoughts.

Others it's lost.

I can see what's real,

and what you pretend,

just by the bubbles,

that float from your head.

Doesn't matter what you choose to say,

these clouds will tell me anyway.

The emotion you have,

and just how deep.

Why your silent,

and what you keep.

The stronger the emotion tied to your words,

is how quickly it's dispersed from your head.

The output.

What's left unsaid.

Some thoughts are stronger,

thicker,

more dense.

Signifies from you,

something really intense.

The emotion attached,

what it repels or attracts.

Some are half whole,

with little pull.

You don't have to say anything you know.

Others thoughts more lovely.

They really glow.

All these circular masses,

showing your molecular classes.

Some faint,

easily pass.

A feeling you had,

that didn't last.

Some so dim,

look rather grim.

All depends on the feelings your holding in.

Thoughts are things.

Rest assured.

To me you don't speak with just your words.

What's best for you to know

are your intentions though.

The universe catches your every blurb.

Just because you think it,

doesn't mean it's not heard.

SPIRITS

Spirits come that do live after,

reach us now by spinning faster.

Take care as you do.

Choose well,

and no harm can come to you.

They can't tell you what to do.

But they will surely guide you,

to what's best for you.

WHISPER

Whisper me a witness,

for all I have been told.

Let me live my life today,

bright,

beautifully,

and bold.

Keep me young,

and my soul always old.

Let what I know inside,

someday,

somehow be known.

Let them see a difference in me.

All I know be shown.

Guide me through my darkest place,

feed me from afar.

Help me to always see that bright so shiny star.

Join me in the end,

let me know I did okay.

Remind me gently,

of what I wished this day.

GHOSTS

When ghosts wake you up at 3 am,

they won't let you be.

They want to be heard and seen,

just like you and me.

When you try to ignore them,

you open up doors.

Ones that may not have ever

existed before.

Inside yourself,

they will invoke,

find a way to provoke,

what they hope.

It's best to just listen.

To hear them out.

Rather than hide and bury yourself.

They're not so bad,

you will discover.

Maybe they just want to say "Hi"

to an estranged lover.

Let someone know,

of an unborn brother.

Give a blessing,

from a grandmother.

A confirmation.

Or revelation.

You'll understand something

in translation.

SKELETON

I came into this lifetime with a skeleton on my
back.

He would climb up and down my spine.

Just like that.

He came to remind me,

of the discomfort I carried.

The one inherent,

with wearing a human body.

This burden of my bag of bones,

wrapped all up

around my soul.

I never liked the feeling you know.

But I came back here to help you grow.

I could've stayed on the other side.

Stayed there to have been a guide.

But I chose to come back.

And the skeleton

wasn't going to let me forget a choice like that.

FAITH

You would be blinded by the light if you knew the

whole truth.

Blown into pieces,

not even exist.

Not down here,

in this world as it is.

You cannot know it all.

You must live humbly,

with all you do know.

Have faith in the journey.

That in time you'll be shown.

Have faith in love,

and for how you'll grow.

Gracefully live,

by all that you know.

The truth is too big for you alone.

Pieces and parts are everywhere.

Have faith in it.

That it is there.

The truth is something we all share.

Know your living it because you care.

Your faith can get you anywhere.

EMOTIONS MY DRUG

My emotions,

how they set me free.

Invigorate.

Intensify,

and intoxicate me.

The unspoken gestures.

The unseen forces.

They're more curious to me than what my mind

is.

Emotions my love.

To feel is my drug.

You are emotions for me to love.

How do you feel about that?

Are you open to the unseen strings?

This is what I watch for,

this is what I bring.

Feel.

Let me see you.

Are you capable?

At every moment we are feeling something.

My first focus,

is how you feel.

The very clues to why you are you.

The way they shape you,

and sometimes break you.

How do you know what you can't feel?

Emotions can be dangerous,

even deadly at times,

but they certainly do make my world chime.

No emotions,

no measure of love.

No way to know why or how deeply we love.

We know we love when we feel joy.

The measure of love?

When pain and hurt does that love bring.

I want to know how you love.

In what ways your love grows or dissipates.

I could be wrong for the way I am,

what I look for,

what I bring.

But my goal is to know the real you.

I love a feeler,

I really do.

Emotions my drug,

are they yours too?

SCRATCHING I

So translucent is my skin.

I'm revealing all the emotions again.

The truths of my heart,

I'm bearing my soul.

Can they see like me,

all I'm too scared to show?

BEING

I feel complete, yet disconnected.

Scattered, yet whole.

Married, yet unborn.

I equal nothing and everything.

I understand the contradiction.

The great simple truth.

The profound allowance to be.

The complicated unending intricate decline of our
human-ness into being-ness.

The interwoven inherited thoughts this world is
full of.

What we get stuck in when trying to escape
them and how hard that can be.

How does this vision of wholeness held within
then be free?

Maybe the freedom is just in knowing that I am
already whole.

What I found out has simply made real what I

always thought I was.

Nothing else seems to matter.

COMPLETE

It was a wind that made me tremble.

Tears seeped from the bellowed corners of my

eyes.

It enhanced everything I felt.

It hit me like a cold wave rolling in from the

ocean.

I became fluid.

I felt all in pieces.

As if I was drifting across this land with no

destination.

Yet totally in sync with what was,

and forever will be.

Complete.

In my incomplete form.

Any questions I had,

became null and void.

It mattered no more.

Almost robbed of my human-ness.

SCRATCHING II

It's just another crazy ride in my reality of the
unconscious.

The biggest
mistake you could
ever make is
being too scared
to make one.

— m.

THE WRITER

There is something so raw and beautiful,

about words first written on blank paper.

The environment to which they cater.

Giving life to something greater.

A magical incantation,

of an emotional translation.

How the stories told,

hold an essence.

A wild leak of magical transcendence.

The dance of creation.

The tracing of shapes,

watching the letters all fall into place.

Before you know it,

a sentence is made.

Forming words,

into something you may have never heard.

Fallen together,

with delicate grace.

Capturing something,

you could never replace.

A productive medium,

for catching it all.

The living,

breathing,

feeling of emotions song.

Readers feeling it's meant effect,

as they follow along.

The vulnerability of its rapture.

Is everything,

that a writer can capture.

ESSENCE

Never erase anything,

you will destroy its essence.

Follow it along on its path.

Write the whole sentence.

If you must rid it of a word,

of which you've heard,

draw a line through it.

Don't erase what could be truth in it.

You may have to go back.

Retrace it's thought,

before it's lost.

You don't want to lose track,

or mistakenly lack,

what may have been taught to you,

within this craft.

The misplacement of a word,

or maybe the thought,

of it sounding absurd,

the easier to understand,

read word.

Better the ones,

everyday heard words.

To convey to them,

the easiest way.

These are the ways,

that a writer plays.

THE HEALER

I can sense what you feel,

see with my eyes the pain you hold,

trapped deep inside.

I can hear what you think,

what you not want me to know.

I can see deep within your very soul.

I can calm you within,

if you would let me in.

These words,

listen well...

The secrets,

the pain,

the truth you do not know.

I am sorry,

but it shows.

What all wants to be hid,

kept within.

You will soon know cannot.

For you must be taught to let go.

Your teacher you see,

is the self you feel lurking within,

nagging your heart.

The one that you would not so willingly,

choose to know.

But you see my friend,

it is more than you think.

I have come here to tell you of this link,

that links you at one with I.

You see,

the pain you feel,

it can be healed.

It is pain none have gone without.

On this earth we walk the path.

A path toward our one true home.

The path is our teacher.

Our teacher,

ourselves.

The knowledge of self takes us home.

The earth our mother,

has lent us her soul.

To show us the truth we all must know.

She has begun,

you see,

trying to tell thee.

The anger,

the pain,

it is destruction.

Not only of her but of ourselves.

It is time to see this now.

It is time to seek what we all must reach.

It is time to know your very own soul.

This journey is long.

A hard path to go.

This I can tell you,

for I know.

But there is no need to hide behind walls,

and the self you have created.

Underneath,

is the seed of your true self.

It seeks for you.

It wants you to know,

the truth it holds.

The time has come to nurture that seed.

Feed and watch it grow.

To discover my friend,

what self could only know.

It is here.

The time,

to part with your fears.

Mourn the pains which have been born within.

You see,

life isn't the mystery,

the mystery is you.

You are a puzzle that must be solved.

And the solver must you.

It is the only way you can go home,

the only way you can be free.

It cannot be up to me.

Though I may want to cure your soul,

be the one to make you whole,

you must know your will,

your way,

yourself.

I can help you see what you need to feel.

Help you feel,

what you need to see,

and in this way help you heal.

Lend a hand on your journey home.

But the task is truly yours.

I can watch and feel your pain with you,

and with this you will gain what is release.

An empty out,

a tender tug in your war to one.

And one you will see,

is no mystery.

It is the link that connects you directly to me.

And to all that is.

This you will see,

this you will know.

When you can find and see,

your true being,

your soul.

You my friend are special,

you'll know.

SOULMATES

You're all my soulmates.

You're all my soul.

We're all made up of the same thing you know.

We're all blended.

All of the time.

There is no real or definite line.

There is,

but it's in your mind.

Energy is all we are.

We're are all so near,

yet still,

so far,

from knowing the truth of who we are.

You're all my soul.

THE DREAMS

Once upon within your dreams,

you will dream what are higher dreams.

You will wonder,

and you'll ask,

what it is,

that's your higher task.

Will you have the ability?

Can you grasp?

What's been placed before you,

on your path?

PLACES

Many places do exist,

past this dimension and far beyond.

In your dreams they do live on.

Quietly hiding,

helping you along.

JUPITER

I used to see Jupiter,

sometimes Mars.

I've even kissed Angels under stars.

Been taught wisdom by sages.

Learned the secrets of love,

and all it graces.

Even been touched by holy faces.

However devastated I am to wake,

over and over again in this place.

There is an alliance,

I can't forsake.

Yet,

still sometimes,

the pain here,

for me is too great.

AWAKENING

There are places I have found,

in the silence past the sound.

Beautiful things can happen you see.

Surely they can,

they have happened to me.

I could tell you of them,

I could try,

but surely words cannot describe,

the wondrous things that you could find,

if you choose to enlighten,

and expand your mind.

Awaken conscious,

within your sleep,

travel places,

where you will meet,

where you can learn,

how to see,

to open up and to live life consciously.

You could feel your body,

all as light,

gracefully fly off,

into the night.

The light is your breath.

You feel so complete.

You know your heart,

as its gentle beat.

You know your love,

you effortlessly feel.

You know its truth,

its power to heal.

Your soul,

you will know,

the freedom it holds.

You know no limits.

They do not exist.

You know all of your lives

and why you've thrived.

You know that truly,

you do not die.

You look at the world from a different view,

with the complete,

whole self.

The other you.

Something down here,

you may never have been able to do.

You will know all your love,

and what is you,

and that you are a keeper

of God's kingdom too.

Well that sums up where you could be,

if you choose to open up

and to live life consciously.

DISTRACTION

If there's a distraction,

I accept its invitation.

If there's an alluring image and I catch it,

it's followed by me.

If there's a dance to be danced,

I'd dance it.

If there's a hole to be fallen into,

my curious self would take over and fall.

So you may see why this mountain is taking me

forever.

I wouldn't want to miss a thing.

I want wholeness for you in the knowledge I

bring.

What help would I be if I did not know?

How then could I help anyone grow?

SPIRAL

I am always constant and never stopping.

Always remembering what I have forgotten.

Letting all go as I flow along,

being always my simple song.

I'm gently circling around myself.

Finding compassion and inner wealth.

I'm diving in,

and rising above,

having courage and always love.

Being myself I say so much.

I am self-knowledge and showing trust.

You will view me in different ways,

moving fast or slow some days.

But I am always moving without a doubt.

Moving all I have within me out.

I am a spiral.

the resurrection:

the remembrance of all her

past selves

SILENCE

When I'm sitting in pure silence,

sometimes music plays within my mind.

Strange music.

Music I've never heard before.

Like baby's music.

Forever to remember.

Maybe I'm remembering.

Maybe all the sudden.

Maybe it's a dream,

which some have forgotten.

SCRATCHING III

Now and then,

we ascend.

And sometimes we're

sent right back down here again.

ACCEPTING THE GIFTS

They say it's to make me wise you know,

that hates to fade and loves to grow.

But frustration is all I feel.

It's hard to say anymore what's fake or real.

They tamper with my temper.

So pushing my buttons.

They're making me remember

all I'd forgotten.

Their sacred touch has shattered all illusion.

THE BURDEN

The freedom away from the hours of pain.

Want to drown them dizzy in hurricane.

This burden I carry,

oh so old.

Keeps me walking in this world,

forever feeling alone.

With these ancient stories,

no one's dare told.

GRANDMOTHER MOONLIGHT

Grandmother moonlight upon our ground

showing us that which remains unfound.

With her light

she then creates,

feelings within you that are innate.

When she shines her light

you cannot deny,

the feelings she helps to signify.

You may be unconscious to her power

till that day,

this month,

that hour,

when she shines forth in her full power.

Grandmother moonlight she is so brave.

She creates within you a tidal wave.

She moves your waters,

your intuition.

She then waits

for you to listen.

She is always there creating this in you.

In hopes that one day

you'll dive deeply into

the true nature she resurrects within you.

The unconscious depths of your true you.

CONJURE

There are many ghosts inside my words.

From a past,

they spin back.

From centuries ago.

Other lives.

Why I've kept them,

now I know.

We remember when we are ready.

Clearly able to handle what we claim.

What we once created,

however insane.

And without guilt,

shame or blame.

But now,

I've conjured up this latent anger.

These burning flames,

they fuel me faster.

This opens me up to immediacy.

Calls me from the general intimacy

of my inactivity.

They are asking me to set them free.

They say my voice will carry.

364 YEARS LATER

You just stand there.

Keep your mouth shut and watch me burn.

You don't dare to go against them.

So you live within the lie of their reflection.

Obeying all you hear.

Dominated by the fear.

I'll keep coming back to remind you

of who you are.

Of that you can be sure.

You turned on me.

And you'll keep turning on me.

Lifetime after lifetime.

Until finally

you will reap what you have sown.

Feel the pain

because you haven't grown.

Always neglecting what you have known.

You'll have to dive deeply

into all you fear to understand.

This is the slight of your own hand.

Being forced into knowing

life's grand plan.

It was your choice to give up your will.

Unconsciously knowing,

it's really you that you killed.

SALEM: THE DREAM

I'm shaking from fear. And my head, I'm not thinking clear. The village people are chasing me. I've been accused. I can see the flickering glow from the light of their torches. It's forcing shadows to dance as they filter through the brakes in objects as they pass by from where I hide.

I'm running from the streets to get protection from the trees. I hear their voices grow louder as they get close. Yet still, it's no match for the sound of my racing heart. I can hear my blood pounding throughout my body. I'm soaked in sweat. I'm scared to death.

As their voices dim down soft, they've moved off into the distance as I get closer to the forest. I turn to see a small body of water hidden in the distance. I must swim. The voices are growing closer to me again. I must cross this lake. I feel the strength of their need to persecute and overpower me. There's this lingering sensation I can feel. It's the grip they could take if I were caught. It suffocates me. I'm fighting to breathe. The darkness in their hearts causes my chest to feel heavy. I'm gasping for air. The affliction they feel, it's not even real. Their bodies are screaming in need of relief. The need to hunt and hurt me. I grow weary. They feel it will save them from a darkness. A darkness breed like disease from word across seas. They are feeding a force they don't understand. It's all been planned. They blindly follow the lead. In killing me they think they will thrive. A masculine, engineered, dominate disguise.

I'm wet from the swim. As I'm walking out from the water I hear a voice.

"There is shelter for you here."

Without a thought and in fear, I race to the voice without hesitation. This man that's spoken has lead me off to a cabin. Momentarily safe, its warm inside. I'm lead to a room off the side from where the fire flies.

"There are fresh clothes for you there." But instead, I walk in and I'm hit upside the head. I awaken later caught. I'm tied up, trapped to a bed.

They are poking at me. There are six of them. Men. Prodding my parts and ripping my skin. Rubbing me in places they should never have been. I can't scream because they've muzzled me. They say the water has rejected me.

From this dominant abuse, I hear that I am the accused.

They've killed me now. Tied ropes around my neck and squeezed me dead.

I no longer have a body.

I birthed babies into the world. I knew of medicines from plants to cure the ill. My touch has warmed the weary. I saw clearly. I held space for sorrows. Brought life back into many someone's dark nights. I know what I'd done in that life's been right.

They think they have dammed me to hell. They called me witch. But I forgive them all this. And everything that had been done to me. My heart is intact. I left that life still a compassionate empath.

<u>PAN</u>

He came to me one night you know.

That half man,

that half goat.

He was as confident as he could be.

His energy strong,

yet filled with peace.

Full of knowledge,

and all he keeps.

He was so quiet,

quite entrancing.

I could feel my insides,

silently dancing.

In some strange way,

he was quite romancing.

Hoof to chin he spoke to me.

What he wanted

was for me to see.

To awaken something wild

within me.

I intently listened to all he told.

In many ways it was all so old.

He came to me at a time when my life was rough.

A stirring up

and removing of all my earthly dust.

Somehow

he confirmed and completed this process.

I was able to move on with all gains and losses.

The goat foot God he lives in you,

someday he may come,

and show you too.

WISH

There's a cherished wish there.

Do you see it?

It's crystal coated.

Been duly noted.

Hidden in the show.

It's been beautiful.

Left there hidden within the gold.

Forever kept whole.

Don't disturb it.

It's like a fairy or a firefly.

Its delicate fibers are purely shy.

Its innocent truth,

you cannot deny.

Unable to be taken by you or I.

So leave the wish cherished.

THE WITCHING HOUR

It is now when most of the world sleeps,

that I sit.

Contemplate.

Think deep.

When I display my grief,

I do sit and weep.

Of what's keeping me from the treasures I keep.

Watching all of those memories re-play,

how I became hardened by them

in some fucked up way.

So I'll keep my treasures locked away,

while my sky is darkened for another day.

Because I can't say.

What do I do with all I hold?

When the emptiness is what I seek.

JESUS

People shaking all around

finding holes within the sound.

Time to awaken,

pay your dues.

Do simply what you've come to do.

Ask me not,

for you can see.

The time has come for you to end your misery.

Tear it out,

twist your within.

Taper down,

and then strip it again.

Ask yourself what you can do.

In many ways,

I'll fly with you.

I AM the one who has come from the sun.

I've carried a lot within my heart.

Now is the time that it must part.

Lost and shelter can no longer be.

You have asked,

now come with me.

I am always walking within your path.

You are my chosen wonder.

I am the one who sits and woos.

You may ask,

well,

who are you?

You cannot tell in the blink of your eye.

I walk with you on the inside.

In your shoes.

I am the one who carries you.

You are my earth and I your water.

Break away and feel your pain.

I am here.

Accept that always.

I am hidden beneath your weak.

Come through now,

I am waiting for you.

No longer harbor beneath your shelter

There's lots here for us to do.

I am waiting.

I've been walking with you.

THE MAP OF LIVES

The map of lives so thoroughly planned.

In my memories that I have scanned.

My thoughts are ever flowing.

Something inside of me,

keeps growing.

Showing.

As the starry sky lingers above,

in time,

I'd hoped to be the dove.

But masks are fading and so's the love.

If I ever make it there

above,

I'm sure I'll wonder what I should have done.

But time is short here.

Mysteries abound.

Maybe next time,

if I come back down.

It will be further embedded in me.

All the lives of my souls' journey.

Enough to know I cannot hold.

Enough to know,

it's ok to be bold.

I won't wonder and you'll just know.

It truly is so strange.

The way we see all things down here.

The way we are all so wrapped in fear.

Paranoia is so loud.

What I had found,

and then gave up.

It's entirely so fucked up.

The things I'm saying,

the things I'm doing.

I'm not even being me at all.

I'm so not confused.

It's easier this time to believe.

It's easier this time,

I see all of me.

I'll just have to integrate all of these personalities.

I truly do know what I know.

Crystal clear it always was.

Crystal clear,

I AM LOVE.

What a strange way for one to see.

By adopting all your past lives personalities.

ONE GREAT LESSON

Oh the teacher standing tall.

Looks so bright as he caws his caw.

His message loud,

currently clear.

You intently listen to all you hear.

All your answers in his eyes,

and all he says,

you'll stand by.

But don't forget what comes inside.

For you truly are your own best guide.

All you have,

what whispers in you,

will lead you gently,

to what's true for you.

So as you listen,

remember you.

Hear his wisdom,

what calls to you.

He is a guide who's helping you,

that's true.

But when it comes down to what's best for you,

no one knows.

Only you.

GENERATION INFORMATION

You are young

and I know you well.

You are living within their hell.

Trying to escape all that you see

and all they tell you,

you should be.

You ran wild all of the time.

Trying to escape what's within their minds.

Trying to make them see what's you.

Holding your vision

of what you know to be true.

Fighting them

every step of the way.

Not listening to what they say.

Rebelling against

all that surrounds.

Because what you feel

is so profound.

You try to show them what you see.

The information that you heed.

You try to wake them from their dream.

Show them there is an in between.

You are you

and that is all.

You are not here to catch where they fall.

You're not they're dreams.

You've come with your own.

You're being yourself.

They think they know,

they think they have the answers.

But what they have,

has caused us disaster.

You just want respect and to be heard.

To know your offering to our world.

Listen to me and hear yourself.

You are our future.

You have come with help.

Keep on going.

Join your hands.

You may not have of what they ask,

but they're still hiding behind their masks.

So you break them

you shake from their dead.

You show them what's hidden within their head.

You're all mirrors for them,

you see.

You will take them back

to reality.

You are our warriors.

You mean them no harm.

You will all make them be one,

and disarm.

Mostly hidden,

you're staying inside.

But who you are you cannot hide.

Your mask is thin,

not like theirs.

You are the ones who took on the dare.

Come out and show us,

have no fear.

There is a reason why you are here.

You may not remember why right now,

but you will someday,

I know somehow.

You may not see,

what it is that you keep.

You may have buried it.

Hidden it deep.

But life has a way of showing us things,

please stay open to the answers you bring.

You're here to answer a prayer.

You are the ones who really care.

I was once just like you,

then I found out when I grew,

just what it was

I'm here to do.

I am hoping that you will see,

beyond the misery and tragedy.

Watch yourself and listen deep,

you will be shown

the answers that you keep.

Don't judge yourself.

Don't live their fears.

Understand that they show

only what they know.

They want to be heard just like you.

So open up,

and listen to them too.

Not only with words but with your heart.

You are the new teachers,

that's part of your heart.

They'll learn from you.

You've come to show them all they can do.

So you keep on listening,

and watching your dreams.

Remember that life is not all that it seems.

You've come with information we all need.

the darkness:

meeting her shadow

SHADOW

I was never afraid of anything.

That's what happens when you've been dead.

And then,

I discovered my shadow.

MY SHADOW

Evil are you?

That's what they say.

When I invoke you out to play.

You're so solid.

Grounded here.

Intimidating,

you generate fear.

You protect me you think.

More often than not

you express yourself when I drink.

When I'm angered or threatened, and

spilling ink.

Yes you are my chaos most days.

But you are also my brave.

You hold and cradle all my pains.

You've made them yours.

Because it's what I have chosen to ignore.

You're a Saint that's been shamed.

The one whom everybody is able to blame.

I now understand

and recognize the game.

Where once I was intolerant,

cast you off to the dark,

I now understand you as a glorious part of my

heart.

You hold such power.

You're a forceful destruction.

Something that at its core

you're doing that's loving.

You're a magically infected,

most curious invention.

My veneer of protection.

A smoke and mirrors

creative maker of manifestation.

I realize now

I need to know the things you know.

I need you to grow.

Because you hold all the shadows in my soul.

THE DREAM BEFORE THE DARKNESS

I was in an airport rushing back out to the parking lot to retrieve something from my car. When I arrived the door was unlocked, but I didn't think anything of it. Just that it was odd. I knew I had to hurry back so that I didn't miss my plane. Security had held onto my purse. When I got it back I looked to see that nothing had been taken. It was the security guy himself who told me to hurry along before I missed my plane.

With my purse in hand, I hurried to the gate where I had to board my plane but on the way, I was stopped by a woman who told me about my destination. I listened intently because I didn't know where I was going myself. She gave me instructions. She said that when I got to London, I was to walk down the dark hall immediately. She spoke as if she was sent to be my guide. Somehow, to help me survive. It was more than just a warning. She gave me instructions.

She said, "Not many are allowed to walk down the dark hall and most don't make it out.

You cannot touch the floor and do not let anyone touch you. Have no fear, stay with your faith"

I looked at her, stunned, as I continued to hurry along.

I was nervous because I didn't understand how I was supposed to go down a dark hall and not touch the floor or its sides or have any sort of physical guide. What made me even more nervous was that not many made it out. I wondered what I had been chosen for. Why did I have to do this and what was its purpose?

I got on my plane and safely, I landed in London.

When I arrived, I got off the plane and immediately saw the dark hall she spoke of. Its darkness reminded me of the kinds of hells I've heard described in various religions and by different people I've talked to about such topics.

It was dark. I could hear loud, creepy snarling voices. I was terrified to enter. I wondered how I was going to go to walk down the hall and not touch the floor. It didn't seem possible. Though I didn't want to, I knew I had to enter.

I began walking toward the hall to the entrance. Just as I was entering I began to float. It was as though I had naturally had this ability and somehow it instantly came back to my memory. I didn't know how it was happening, I just knew I was relieved. There were hands reaching out at me from the darkness. They were trying to grab me. I wanted to let them. I felt I could help them. I felt I could take away their pain and grief. All their anger and cries, but I remembered that I would instantly die. And still, I wanted to help them, but I heeded what I had been told. I kept moving. I did not let them touch me. I couldn't let their darkness get to me.

I woke up. And then, the darkness came.

I didn't know why then that I had that dream, or why most are not allowed to go into the dark hall. I woke up feeling like I had been chosen to do something most others had not. Going to London may have been a metaphor for the dark hall being foreign territory to me. The darkness, the scary unknown. The hands, my relationship to others. I understand not being able to touch the ground and instantly having the ability to float, as an unknown or unconscious strength that exists within myself that I will find if I'm brave enough to leap. It could also mean the ability to call back to myself when necessary the strengths I have had in any lifetime. I must trust in what I cannot see. "Have no fear, stay with your faith" is about believing in myself and my faith. The hall itself, a walk alone in a darkness that feels like hell. I believe this is why this statement was made that "Not many make it out." I wasn't so sure I was going to.

As I woke from the dream, the Lord's prayer came to my mind.

"Even though I walk through the valley of the shadow of death, I will fear no evil, for you are with me; your rod and your staff they comfort me."

SCRATCHING IV

There's a flowing freedom that's hidden from you.

Stealing footsteps,

unaware is you.

EGO

As you began your journey to you,

there are many shadows you must walk through.

Ones that keep you from you.

The ones we find

inside our mind.

Like the ego.

The one that won't let go.

The one that does not want you to grow.

The many tricks it will play on you.

The many lessons it hopes you won't learn,

for the life of things

that it still yearns.

The surrender,

it can't.

It won't let you know.

For the truth would fade it,

would cause it to grow.

The silence it fears,

would be its death.

It fears it will then

be put to rest.

It does not want life wondrous and grand.

It does not want you to expand.

It likes its games.

It's triggering ways.

For you to believe just what it says.

The ego is not without its purpose.

It is truly here for us to learn.

It helps us know what it is to be human.

Feeling so fully this place that we dwell in.

Makes it real,

so we truly feel.

The ego blocks our vision and casts an illusion.

It is its game,

and it likes to play.

One day your ego will be quiet,

and decide to let you walk on by it.

Surrender yourself (ego) to be yourself.

SHAME

I'm confronting a darkness I have yet to claim.

Who knew that darkness' name

could be shame.

And that it really wasn't

all me I had to blame.

I'm sinking into it.

Feeling its truth.

I found shame way back,

disguised in youth.

Shame hid who I really was.

Shame took away the feeling of love.

Shame sent a part of myself to darkness.

Kept it secret.

Played victims game.

Shame started placing blame.

Shame grieved my uniqueness

because she was taught it was weakness.

Shame tried to cast away my sensitivity.

Tried to leave me exposed.

Shame named vulnerability frailty.

Shame became its own entity.

Living as an aspect

of my personalities.

As I walked down the valley of all this mess,

I waited in the shadow.

So that I could meet with the creature shame.

To understand from where she came.

She was just a little girl.

Shame nestled itself down deep in her brain.

Shame taught her to be a people pleaser.

Shame did everything

so that people wouldn't leave her.

I'm not good enough is what shame taught.

With pleasing actions love must be bought.

Be a good girl.

Whatever their perspective.

Anything less

you'll be left in wreckage.

I need to integrate shames lesson of hurt.

Include it somehow into my own self-worth.

Illuminate shame from the shadow with grace.

Release the false people pleasing face.

SCRATCHING V

They will do anything to shame you into being the
same you.

Didn't think shame worked that way did you.

They will feel your rising and they will pull you
back.

Snap.

And just like that.

You'll retract.

You'll start to feel slightly attacked.

It's something they are unaware that they do.

Unconsciously

they will kill off pieces of you.

Unless,

you make every effort to see yourself through.

<u>FEAR</u>

I saw myself alone in darkness again.

Floating in water.

Completely black.

It felt so empty.

So all alone.

There were no connections

to my soul.

I heard the words.

It still hurts.

I met a fear.

Suddenly,

it all became clear.

Why I felt dead.

Only in darkness could I have made the

discovery.

That everyone's breathe

I had cut off from me.

In this disconnection,

I felt connection.

When alone in darkness,

was all I was left with.

Self-reflection I went in.

DIXON

Meet me.

Match me.

Show me your teeth.

But the truth is below you and you don't

understand the underneath.

Have a dog?

A dazzling Dixon?

Anything in which you keep your wish in?

Guess you'll have to dig to your roots.

Get muddy,

them pretty rubber boots.

Keep me your friend or make me your foe.

I'll still show you what you need to grow.

Either way,

you sent for me.

I'm not the one choking your free.

And in no way are you bound to me.

Let it go.

You know better in your soul.

104 *shelby lalonde*

THE STRUGGLE IS REAL

The struggle is real.

You mean what you created and cannot heal?

Or shit of which you just can't deal?

This struggle you speak of,

do tell.

I grow curious of its nature.

What's that?

It's just an expression?

Or affirmation I say.

These are dangerous words with which you play.

KOOL-AID GIRLS

They all drink the same Kool-Aid

them girls you know.

The drifters.

The non-independent thinkers.

The *easily swayed* girls.

Always listening to what the *others say* girls.

Their need to be accepted.

Their need to *think like them* girls.

Even when they *know better* than

to pretend girls.

The go back and *do it all again* girls.

Before they know it,

they are the *lost girls.*

Totally *rocked off their path* girls.

Even the ones who think they aren't.

Slowly,

they are *the ripped apart* girls.

ENDLESSLY

Don't think I'm unaware

that you've crossed a line.

Many lines.

For the sake of being kind,

to build you up,

I let it be.

I sacrifice me.

I don't know why I do

what ultimately feels best,

only for you.

Oh wait,

yes I do.

I feel like I'm helping you.

And now you feel for a moment better than me.

Good luck.

Endlessly.

No amount of competition will set you free.

It's fucking insanity.

Realize it's a lesson.

No matter,

that your ego's pretending.

Barely defending its kindergarten perception.

FRIEND

You were my friend and I love you,

no matter what has happened between us two.

I'll always hold you close to my heart,

for now,

and as long as we remain apart.

Our egos will die,

as our souls find home,

and what's come between us now

will then be gone.

You are still my friend.

I'll always love you.

SCRATCHING VI

I can see the pieces of myself that I've scattered

and sprinkled into the people I know.

One's that together we've grown.

I feel like I've lost my identity though.

It's slipped away to them somehow you know.

Did I give of myself to much?

This mirror image,

I'm supposed to trust?

These pieces of myself that I miss so much?

How do I replace?

Maybe I've replaced them,

in some unknown way.

Created new,

allowed them to slip away.

After all,

I'm wanting to grow.

Been pushing out

and away with the old.

ALONE

I am alone.

There's no one who stands behind me

or beside me.

No one who's going to defend me or define me.

I had a circle.

It crumbled to the ground.

As much as it devastated me,

something about this is freeing to me.

Empowering even.

Today with great clarity comes the realization.

I can trust no one,

but I must trust myself.

In this discourse,

I am now able to see my course.

SCRATCHING VII

I'm not lost,

I'm experiencing uncomfortable feelings.

LIGHTNING

My mind seems not so vast.

Something in my heart has been long collapsed.

As my essence seeps away,

my moonlit carriage lingers.

Lost in mud puddles,

stuck now,

in the murky visions that I keep hidden.

Lost to all its sensitivity and inner wisdom,

I can't see through

because the lightening right now

seems so frightening.

The flashes of light with my eyes closed tight.

The colors,

it's energy won't go away.

Still its journey escapes me.

The carriage casts me free from everything I was

sent to be.

I can't invite my divinity.

Live up to it with integrity.

How do I zero in on any one of its possibilities?

I guess it's that lightening.

It's a blink of the physical eye.

Seen in a flash,

recognized,

just like that.

I'll catch it before it escapes,

into something my heart can't yet navigate.

Wait.

I find I fixate.

GLOW

What I relate to you anymore I do not know.

It's all seemed to drizzle down deep to my toes.

I can't feel the mystery.

I can't see the glow.

My hope has been showered

all out from my soul.

It's in a pool at the bottom.

It simply keeps.

It's been frozen now at my feet.

It rests asleep.

It doesn't move or even weep.

It's like a picture created.

Looks like glass.

The kind that you can't ever see through or past.

To transparent,

too thick to grasp.

Rich with emotions that's pooled up fast.

For all these devoted divisible paths,

I can't feel my face.

Nor can I erase my faith.

Looking for where,

it's been lost or misplaced.

Within what's been frozen,

now here below in my space.

I remember how I fell,

all too well.

SELF-TALK

That beauty is not lost.

Its lingering in you.

Capture it back.

Here's a clue for you.

THE SORCEROUS

Angels vengeance being brought down on me.

Everything so clearly

I'm unable to see.

Heaven has bestowed these gifts onto me.

Seems they've released them to generously.

Can they take back what once they'd given?

Am I,

the unforgiven?

It's me.

Myself,

I think that keeps me.

When once before,

I felt so freely.

For now,

I'm bound.

My inner sorcerous cannot be found.

SCRATCHING VIII

Mad at myself for *sleeping* with you,

When *awakening* you is what I came here to do.

RESERECTION

You can raise the dead.

Sure you can.

But you must kill yourself first.

Destroy your identity.

Turn your bones towards the earth.

Engulf yourself,

in the open pyer.

Burn away everything you desired.

Fall into the emptiness of your captivity.

Meet eye to eye,

with why you seek what you seek.

Go to your own hell.

Where your ego dwells.

Rediscover,

what you have covered.

And what you thought would make you whole.

You can raise the dead you know.

ALCHEMY

As my weight shifts,

I sit.

I wait here.

For it to appear.

I alchemize the fear.

I drift.

As my light tends to the darkness of all this,

I don't know what to say.

It's another mystery that's being revealed to me

this way.

CYCLES

I'm in a low cycle.

Sometimes these cycles last years.

I search for answers

within the tears.

I find cycles within the cycles.

I tell myself to let it be.

Go on.

Keep living life adventurously.

But it's hard for me to accept any one cycle of

unproductivity.

Your desire for change must be greater than your

need to stay the same.

Impermanence is Imperial.

HABIT

This repetition is choking me.

Suffocating my vulnerability.

Not maturing the mystery.

I want my wild and divine unpredictability.

To walk on waves.

The bygones of being brave.

That's the stuff that takes my breathe away.

The mundane to me

feels like chains.

The habitual,

the habits.

I've grown bored with it now.

I've got to find my way out of this somehow.

GOOD AND BAD

What's good?

What's bad?

All of those feelings that I have had.

Who will tell me,

who will say?

What is it really anyway.

Would I be the evil of all this world?

Is it I,

who all have feared?

Would I be the Angel who all would say,

the one who's come to save the day?

What is it really anyway?

If you were to ask me,

what would I say?

I'd say I'm both all wrapped in one.

What would the world do with me then?

What is it really anyway?

What would they say?

If they looked within themselves they will see,

they are not unlike you or me.

Let's not be separate,

not anymore.

Open up from within,

the door that hides our humanness.

The one that lets no other see,

what is really,

our reality.

We are all the same deep down within.

Let now be the time that we begin.

Open up ourselves for others to see,

we really live the same reality.

Rise above what's good what's bad.

What is a really anyway?

the integration:

the merging of all her selves

UNDERWORLD

As I stand at the edge of the underworld,

I discover that goodness is a cover.

What made you want to be good?

And please define it if you would?

EVERMORE

He waited while my wings were so swiftly held.

Clipped,

within my own grip.

I was tarring through my evermore.

Opening up

every dark door.

Till I found myself safe

at a glorious shore.

Bound,

I would be no more.

SUICIDE BRIDGE

Yes.

The suicidal thoughts seeped into my existence.

This is where I found myself

fighting with resistance.

This wasn't me.

Or anything I'd ever believed.

I know this to be a personal sin.

I who have come back here

over and over again.

I needed to figure out how I could want to live

again.

The deepest cries,

I called out to myself.

Because no one around me

could understand the needed help.

I totally knew,

I'd have to rely on me

and my higher-self.

Thing is,

I had snubbed her out.

Awakened my shadow,

I was drunken with doubt.

All I could be

was cleverly covered up by me.

I had turned my back,

on what I was about.

I abandoned her guidance.

I killed what I knew.

This is why,

it was to her I had to get through to.

She alone,

would know what to do.

I just had to reach her frequency.

Let her back into my existing reality.

So I searched and I searched for that one divine
line.

The one that I knew

that was heard every time.

That part of myself,

who wore compassion and held divine wealth.

So I tracked myself back.

I knew that I owed to her that.

To also myself,

and to everyone else.

I found there were others along the way.

There were others there,

in myself at play.

The egos magician,

she's hard to persuade.

But I pushed through her in every way.

My higher self

yelled for me to be brave.

I knew I heard her.

That is all I can say.

It was all so terrifying really.

But I picked up a pen,

and I let myself begin to bleed again.

This was her gift.

My counselor indeed.

My higher self,

that I was in need.

The pen was the only way I could never hide.

The real me came through it every time.

That I could never disguise.

With the pen in my hand

I was shown.

I was never once left here alone.

It's no wonder I hadn't used it.

Disregarded myself,

because I couldn't see into it.

I told myself I hadn't the strength.

That I was a fool.

To myself I had turned cruel.

Told myself I was destined to fail.

But all the while,

my higher self knew that I would prevail.

I just kept crying,

to help myself please.

So then she came to me

in my dreams.

In meditation,

and when my pen did bleed.

It was her reflection,

All I could see.

Her reflection,

that reflected myself back to me.

I was able to get myself on the right track.

The more I opened up,

the more she talked back.

I gave her my time.

I gave her my space.

Her love came in,

with abundance and grace.

She soon filled up with love,

that horrible place.

I then saw her in everyone's face.

She was in the people that I love the most,

that's what really

resurrected her ghost.

In I,

her human host.

She is me.

I was able to integrate her back into me.

I needed to be on suicide bridge.

To again appreciate,

that this lie is a gift.

THE OTHER SELVES

Sometimes it's like seeing yourself fall away.

Like watching someone else take over.

Like wearing something unfamiliar.

Not quite comfortable,

yet exciting somehow.

We set pieces of ourselves on the shelf for a while,

so that the others may experience,

explore.

Adventure

where we once ignored.

THE OTHER SELVES PART 2

There are all these personalities

living inside of this one me.

They interact,

they entertain,

they play an awful dramatic game.

I learned to listen

where I hadn't before.

I've recognized what all of the fighting's been for.

They've been ignored.

As I now stand by and let them be,

all aspects of my personality.

I listen to them now,

so tenderly.

In essence,

I've learned to set them free.

By accepting all aspects of my personality.

I've integrated them into one me.

136 *shelby lalonde*

I learned to see,

by accepting all points

as validity.

Where once before,

they were so loud.

Back and forth with answers,

no common ground.

As this chaos proceeded in me

I recognized also,

something else.

They were mirroring energies,

outside of myself.

Their voices often echoed what others would say.

I had internalized the games being played.

I was able to handle this chaos now,

in a different way.

For what I saw in someone else,

I now searched for inside of myself.

This helped the relationship I had with myself.

If you don't listen your other selves,

how can you listen to anyone else?

If you fight with the others inside of yourself,

how can you not fight with anyone else?

My suggestion then is for you to find a way

to get along with all of them.

Every one of them inside and outside

is a part of you.

They all are needing your attention too.

So don't suppress them.

Take into consideration all that they speak.

If you don't,

you'll remain incomplete.

You'll need to get along with all of your selves

before really getting along

with anyone outside of yourself.

How will you be able to deal with anyone else,

if you can't first deal with what's inside of

yourself.

EMPTINESS

I've watered through my abundant self.

I felt its wealth.

Though I'm drifting,

the remedy is the emptiness of the everything

that's been stripped.

In the nothingness,

where my heart had stopped.

When there was nothing but darkness.

I remembered before.

In the pitch black madness,

created taverness that came again.

A light I could see.

I recognized this light as me.

This light I had looked for so desperately.

This light has always existed you see.

I found myself the secret.

In the darkest of holes,

I started a fire again

from its coals.

I began to burn.

Not caring what from people I heard.

No expectation.

No shame nor guilt.

I recognized it was my obligation

to build what could be built.

SCRATCHING IX

When there's not enough light to make shadows,

but you see them anyway,

only to realize they are not shadows at all.

Your seeing your life's light through the gift of

its darkness.

You see its energy.

Can feel its nocturnal tone.

Of a place you once had made your home.

The one deep down inside of your ethereal bones.

<u>NOTES</u>

I suppose if I stay here long enough,

some frustrated talent might come through.

That something inside of me

will tell me what I'm supposed to do.

Some hidden agenda I might not know of yet.

Something they've kept.

Something truer than I've ever known.

I feel so surprised as I sit here and look at my

notes.

My scattered be shrewd.

I already knew.

Something inside I find tells me now

what I'm supposed to do.

YOURSELF

Don't tell anyone about yourself.

That version of yourself was yesterday.

You're not the same today.

Every day you change.

The very person you tell about yourself

may be the person who changes you.

Let them see you.

Don't tell them.

Show them instead.

To speak of yourself,

is risky.

You limit yourself to living within the confines of

your own words.

An exact description of what's been already

heard.

You tie yourself to an imaginary tree.

Even an emotion maybe.

This is of no benefit to anyone you see.

Least of all yourself.

We die and are reborn every day.

INTEGRATION

Facing your darkness creates light.

Generates life.

Forces you through your dark night of the soul.

To the integration,

that can make you whole.

Here,

you can defeat your fears.

Face all your selves

and all the lies you've told yourself.

Your shadow consists of what you think is good

too.

Latent talents you may have never used.

Awaiting there,

are gifts for you.

So process through what you have repressed.

Awaken yourself to what you reject.

Open up to what you regret.

You must struggle through

to find out about what's true for you.

To you,

yourself only do you have something to prove.

SOVEREIGNTY: THE DREAM

I saw myself in a lush, full forest floating
naked in midair. Surrounded by a radiant mass of
pink and white light moving in all directions
about 8 feet each way all around me. There were
golden streams of a rain like a substance
flickering itself through me. I watched on in such
awe of this display as my body began to softly fall
to the ground.

I suddenly switched perspective. I, now
inside my body felt refreshed with my spirit
floating vastly expanded around my physical self.

A woman dressed in a black lace dress up
to her neck came walking toward me. She was
definitely not from this century I thought to
myself as she came closer. She was strong I felt.
She had a confidence about her that I could only
ever hope to acquire. This confidence could be
described as self-assurance. Every step she made
seemed to shatter the boundaries of our current
physical existence. Her steps became part of
everything that surrounded us including myself.

She was carrying a large dark book in the clutches of her left arm. She stopped just above my head and said,

"Take my hand, I have something to show you".

I was hesitant. She was intimidating. This was a woman who has embraced her own power. She was responsible for something greater than herself. This I felt. Especially now from where I lay. But I discovered that I trusted her anyway.

So I took her hand as I began to stand. We started walking side-by-side down a path forged through the forest. This forest was different than any forest I have in my memories. It seemed to speak. Reach out for us. As if we were tightly held. It was comforting to feel that something so large, so vast, could be so aware of what was happening inside of me.

As we walked, she talked. She handed me the book she held and she asked me to look inside. I opened it. With one look I felt all of its knowledge now inside myself somehow. As if it had always been there. I just had not been aware.

She said,

"You have to accept this part of yourself. What you think or have been taught to think of as darkness is not. You have to accept the gifts that are waiting for you inside of this book. It is inside yourself."

I asked,

"Do I have to be a witch?"

She replied,

"You are one. Like it or not it's part of who you are and embracing it is wholeness and love for yourself. You must accept the knowledge that you have ignored. You are a healer and record keeper. This book will explain to you what that means and then you must re-define it for yourself. Give it life again. Give yourself life. Your whole self. And after that you must choose the words you use wisely. Redefine them. The world is ready for you now."

As we walked I realized that she was this part of me. An outward manifestation of a part of myself that I have ignored. The moment I realized this, she disappeared. But she wasn't gone. She has always been a part of me. I may have suppressed her but her influence in my life could always be felt.

SCRATCHING X

That I wasn't good enough.

For them?

But it's always been me.

What's this shift in perspective I see?

In sync with the universal symphony?

In loving them,

I can still be free.

But simply,

not let it take life away from me.

I kept myself trapped.

Gave myself an excuse to be simple like that.

I wanted to be just like everybody else.

I wanted to help people feel good about

themselves.

But my responsibility,

greatly,

has always been me.

To first start with loving

every aspect of my own personality.

AS I GLANCED

I look in the mirror this day,

this night.

I see who I am,

what I look like.

But it is not what I saw as I glanced,

now what put me in my trance.

In the mirror I see my face.

The part of me

I made for this place.

I know this in my heart so dear.

This part of myself became so clear.

I seen true beauty as I glanced.

My heart jumped up and began to dance.

My beauty is further beneath my skin.

In all the truth I hold therein.

It is my soul that speaks within my heart.

My heart is bigger than I can see.

I remain unconscious to this part of me.

But all the beauty I hold within,

now is the time I must bring it in,

to this world in which we live.

It's time to fly,

to gain my wings.

This is the truth my heart shall sing.

This is the truth from my soul to my heart,

the promise I gave

to do my part.

<u>FIRE</u>

Tragic,

I have to solidify the ashes.

Though the fire has endangered my soul,

I have to make my presence known.

Somehow,

I must make this fire my home.

Live in the heat.

Dance in the fire.

Ignite the ability to transform my desires.

In human modesty,

somethings insane.

My pleasures,

my pain,

what's inexplicably sane.

Disaster subsides.

There's a fool in all our eyes.

I'm going to catch its wisdom.

I choose to eat the forbidden.

I've fought through every frailty,

every human curve.

Every time the circle cycled back my way,

I made movement.

I have my Angels to help me through,

they are beside me in all I do.

However tragic what I do may seem to you.

They keep me aware of the fires I brew.

Watch me closely so I know what to do.

They say I must be brave for you.

That someone's got to.

<u>LEAP</u>

Like something bigger is on the curb.

It walks beside me

waiting to be heard.

Asks for me

to conjure up the nerve.

I'm looking forward.

Too straight to see.

I'm not blind to it.

I'm aware.

And though I'm expanded by its presence,

it has consequences.

There's a responsibility attached.

I've answered it before.

If I accept it,

if I look at it,

there's no turning back this time.

Only one path is fated.

I need to be ready.

Not negate it.

I must be ready when I greet it to leap.

Nothing about this will be discrete.

I'll need my stamina to reach it peak.

MY KIN

I live a life unlike any other.

I'm on the road to what is discover.

Some say my way is cruel and cold,

some say my way is wise and bold.

The things that I have unveiled from within,

have brought me much for you my kin.

Some things that I've seen,

have scared me to death,

but I found my fears,

and put them to rest.

Some things I see,

I love them so much,

and I'm helping that beauty rise up from its dust.

What I have found are my many facets.

I am everything that I have seen.

Outside myself I do exist,

I am everywhere and everything.

I am everything not in my grasp,

and I am everything within it.

I am everything that I see in you,

I am everything I want to be,

and all I don't want too.

How on earth can I be that?

I would never act that way.

I would never,

hear me say.

But as I sit and drift and sway I go deeper.

And I can see that yes this is reality.

It's hard to love yourself sometimes.

To look at things you'd rather not.

Knowing what I know can come with great cost.

Sometimes I feel so all alone.

I could not blame those who choose not to see,

eternally shatter their reality.

All the masks they choose to wear.

The protection they have from themselves.

Sometimes I wish I had them too.

But I made a promise and to keep it.

I promised to help you find you,

and that is what I intend to do.

the rising:

her Venus is on the rise

WOMAN

What do I love?

I love walking barefoot and the smell of wet dirt.

Long skirts,

believing in grace and that its bound within the

earth.

Dancing by firelight,

Clogs...

Foraging foots forth,

crickets chirping,

and every moonlight.

Writing in the night.

Whispering to my babies,

seeing their smiles,

telling them how every raindrop feeds their inner

light.

Pushing through darkness.

Waking in the night.

Meeting my boundaries.

The gifts that call me,

and how in them I found these...

The fears I have to fight.

That darkness equals light.

And what I am here to ignite.

High heels clunking about.

Mysteries,

the puzzles in the solemn hymns I've found.

And most of all,

The woman I am becoming.

And will become.

The waking passion,

I breathe every day.

SHE

She found ways to learn about herself

that's not dependent on anyone else.

She can manifest her every dream.

She is certain that the universe

will follow her every thought and need.

She chooses carefully,

and with absolute certainty.

She has the vision to see.

Recognizes,

so her heart won't bleed.

She does not allow chaos to overtake.

Not in any form or any shape.

Her space is the one thing

she will no longer negotiate.

She's in control

yet she knows

when she needs to follow flow.

She knows she has nothing to fear.

She finally feels safe being here.

<u>TRUST</u>

Trust your heart.

Trust your knowing.

Trust your truth.

Trust your own reality.

It is unique.

It is yours.

And it is truth.

You are a human undefined.

A being in,

and of the divine.

YOUR HEART

What lies within your heart?

Do you know what's there?

Can you listen,

do you dare?

The whispers,

the answers when you ask?

Can you feel your heart telling you?

Have you buried what it's said?

Instead you listen with your head?

All those feelings,

And what you dread?

Are you still listening in your head?

Listen to grow.

What's keeping you?

SHINE

Stop being scared of how strong you are.

We know you know you're not weak.

Put your head up.

Stop fumbling.

Give it your all.

It's okay if you multiple times fall.

We know you feel your protecting others

with what you keep.

But you're not.

You too must be free.

What will protect them,

is letting them see.

So go on now,

shine your light brightly.

THE CRYSTAL CAVE

I wish you would come to the crystal cave,

be awakened in every way.

Know the rainbow and all its rays.

It's quiet message,

what it says.

It's your transcendence,

the crystal you.

The crystal cave,

it belongs to you.

<u>RISE</u>

As I look into the doorways of other worlds,

of what's to come,

and what will pass.

I wonder,

and I think.

I almost want to stay here sometimes.

Leaving all the beauty and peace behind.

To stay here in this world I've so wanted to leave.

I guess it's just showing me.

For I know I must go on.

I guess it's just teaching me,

to love this world where I have been.

To love that which has helped me to grow.

To embrace it all before I go.

I know the beauty that lives within it,

and I know I must never forget it.

I must love this part,

and what's my past,

for a firm future,

and one that lasts.

The time has come for me to rise.

GREAT COSMIC JOKE

I woke up one day within this life,

I was sitting alone in my bed that night.

I woke up knowing it was all just a dream.

Everything.

All that my life has been.

I felt so suddenly the universal scheme.

I was laughing so hard I could barely breathe.

What a big joke I had played on me.

What a big joke this reality.

We really are much bigger than this.

This life seems barely to exist.

I was laughing all in bliss.

How could I have forgotten all of this?

Just wake up.

The time is now.

BUTTERFLIES

We are all like butterflies deep inside.

At a slower pace is the time it takes to see its face.

The face we truly are inside.

Once we get a taste of our true face,

some go on to journey further.

Others stop in their sadness and hide the faces

they reveal.

They build their walls for no kicking down.

Many times

I have seen my fate.

It's like a window to this place.

A place inside my heart and spirit.

The fate that I hold inside my soul,

is a beautiful place where we all live.

It's not a secret where it is.

It's a long and hard the journey there,

to be there all at once as we should be,

who has the key?

174 *shelby lalonde*

We as people I believe.

The soul,

the spirits we all are.

We have the key.

Knock down the walls we once built up,

uncover our faces have no fear.

See the spirits we are so dear.

Find the cocoon and then break through it,

we then become butterflies to all eyes,

hearts and spirits.

CONNECTION

The trees are taller still,

as I glance past this vast hill.

My aching heart is hollow,

yet still,

it is filled.

For every child and spirit I see.

These are the things that connect for me.

SEEKING TRUTH

If you seek the truth you will find it.

But you must learn to recognize it.

Know that we all may not have the same truths.

This does not mean that theirs is wrong and yours

is right or vice versa.

It just means that we are individual beings,

which means we are different.

With our own signature soul.

We all hold our own truths.

All are pieces of the whole truth.

All are valid.

When we know this,

we can grow.

If we find ourselves at judgment here,

ask yourself,

would I want to be judged for my

beliefs?

Sit and search within your soul,

for that piece of empathy.

Open up to understanding another human being.

When you find it,

you will know that you have found a bit of

unconditional love,

that is possible with all that lives.

Every human,

every creature,

animal or star,

no matter who or what they are.

Love is the answer,

love is the key,

to what lies hidden within the mystery.

We can let each other *be*.

Shine forth in your own light,

allow others the same.

You follow that and you will see,

there is simply truth in everything.

FLY

I am going to fly as if I have nothing attached.

I am going to let it all go so that I may be free.

I am going to escape what I think I should be.

I will carefully look when I am stripped,

and then rebuild

as if I am already equipped.

Create as I go,

only that which I choose.

Myself again,

I shall never abuse.

It's not important what anyone thinks.

We're all changing.

All of the time.

Sometimes,

we cycle through.

These cycles that mean so much to you.

If you want to change,

you must break free from the cycles you've held

onto so tightly.

Set yourself free.

Create healthy boundaries.

Learn to be comfortable empty.

ENERGY

I am constantly spinning,

circling,

spiraling,

in and out of me.

This is visible with my eyes

and I can feel my consciousness rise.

Taking me to hidden places within my mind.

Energy of the undefined kind.

This is a blessing.

It is divine.

Bringing me from my darkness to my light.

I thank you God,

Goddess,

and all that is.

I will use this knowledge the best that I can.

I will carry her light until the end.

Giving it,

passing it through me.

Giving what you give eternally.

I will forever be in love with all of you.

Everything you are.

I carry you always in my heart.

For I know now we were never even apart.

THE TIME HAS COME

The time has come,

this day and age to turn the page.

Become one with the self within the body.

The spirit,

the soul,

that lurks inside.

Your will,

the courage to know yourself deep.

To realize there are no secrets to keep.

Denial is one of our greatest teachers.

Own it all,

everything you think you hate.

Navigate your life with courage.

Describe to yourself,

what it's teaching you.

There are many teachers and lessons to know.

Give into it.

Just flow.

Watch yourself grow.

Be conscious of all you let in your space.

Be aware of what lies within,

and how you process it into you.

Take your time,

and be willing to find what you need to grow.

HEAVEN ON EARTH

I dream of the place where you can be.

A place away from chaos and misery.

A place that's filled and ripe with love.

A place you'd say came from above.

A quiet place where you can be.

A place where you will feel no need

to hide behind what you create,

and what they taught you,

you should be.

A place where you can come,

to unwind and come undone.

To empty out and feel yourself.

To bring that self to its birth.

To get all out,

and past the hurt.

To see we came to make us free.

To stop this wheel is our destiny.

To un-trap us from our past,

to make this place,

finally at last,

the heaven they said would be of this earth.

The heaven I know we are meant to birth.

GATEWAY TO ENLIGHTENMENT

Everyone has their own way in which they

become enlightened.

Seeing when they are ready is what they will.

It is not as easy as trying to make one see.

But don't give up on them.

You can do your part by following your heart.

Lead by example from that central space within.

Continue to care.

Open up to all.

Dare to love them anyway.

Be a light in their lives as well of your own.

In this way,

you will show what must be known.

In this way,

you will then be shown

the gateway to enlightenment.

You will have earned the right to re-enter into

real reality.

OUR SLUMBER

We together sleep clasping the promise of

tomorrow.

As the earth and sky mingle in generous gift,

the bounty is ours for secret taking.

We sleep held by the destiny

of our own secret stars.

And so now we will sleep until another dawn.

Waiting to be summoned,

by the destiny

of our own secret stars.

Please visit shelbyllalonde.org for more
information and future titles

Also by Shelby:

When Love Cracks

Coming Soon:

Venus Rising

Shelby L. LaLonde is a strawberry blonde Gemini mystic who loves all things metaphysical. She gardens, loves to dance, and though many know her as a photographer, she will tell you that her true love is to write. Often found spinning tarot, or gazing at the moon, Shelby is a Certified Psychic and Reiki practitioner who remains a member of the International Honor Society having studied at Cazenovia College and Syracuse University. She is a member of the CNY Creative Writers Café. She lives in a small village near Syracuse New York with her husband John the Pisces.

47325529R00123

Made in the USA
Middletown, DE
10 June 2019